SANJEEV KAPOOR

Kabab
Lajawab!

In association with Alyona Kapoor

Popular Prakashan
www.popularprakashan.com

Published by
POPULAR PRAKASHAN PVT. LTD.
301, Mahalaxmi Chambers
22, Bhulabhai Desai Road
Mumbai - 400 026
for KHANA KHAZANA PUBLICATIONS PVT. LTD.

First Published 2013

(4343)
ISBN: 978-81-7991-784-8

Design: Anjali Sawant
Photography: Aarti Manik, Alim Bolar, Bharat Bhirangi, Mangesh Parab, Mukesh Munim and Satish Parab

PRINTED IN INDIA
by Sai Print 'o' Pack
New Delhi - 110 020

AUTHOR'S NOTE

Kabab, a wide variety of skewered appetisers as well as snacks, originating from the Middle East, have quickly been adopted and adapted in various parts of the world including India. In English, kabab generally refers to meat served on skewer; in the Middle East, however, kabab refers to meat that is cooked over or next to flames. The traditional meat for kabab is lamb, but depending on the regional tastes, it may be created from different types of vegetables, goat, chicken and fish.

Various kinds of freshly ground Indian spices are added to the yogurt used for the marinating the meat or the key ingredient of the kabab. Occasionally unripe papaya is used to make it tender. The kababs are usually garnished with mint leaves and served with onions and Indian bread.

Try the kababs in their various avatars like the Bhutta Seekh Kabab, Chicken Makhmali Kabab, Dahi ke Kabab, Galouti Kabab and receive accolades from your friends and relatives.

Happy kabab-making!

CONTENTS

NON-VEGETARIAN KABABS

Vegetable Shaami Kabab

200 grams yam, cut into 1-inch pieces
2 medium potatoes, cut into 1-inch pieces
1 large carrot, grated
10-12 French beans, finely chopped
¼ cup shelled green peas, coarsely ground
4 tablespoons split Bengal gram, soaked
1 teaspoon cumin seeds
1 inch ginger, finely chopped
2-3 green chillies, finely chopped
Salt to taste
2 tablespoons chopped fresh coriander
¼ teaspoon turmeric powder
½ teaspoon *garam masala* powder
½ teaspoon red chilli powder
5 teaspoons lemon juice

1. Drain the Bengal gram and transfer to a non-stick pan.
2. Add the yam, potatoes and one and a half cups of water. Cover and cook till soft and completely dry.
3. Heat another non-stick pan. Add the cumin seeds and roast lightly. Add the carrot, French beans, green peas, ginger, green chillies and salt, and sauté on medium heat for two minutes. Transfer to a plate and set aside to cool.

4. Grind the Bengal gram mixture along with the sautéed vegetables to make a smooth mixture.
5. Add the chopped coriander, turmeric powder, *garam masala* powder, chilli powder, and lemon juice, and mix well. Adjust the seasoning.
6. Divide the mixture into sixteen equal portions and shape into balls. Flatten lightly in the palm of your hand to form kababs. Refrigerate for an hour.
7. Heat a non-stick frying pan and cook the kababs till golden brown on both sides.
8. Serve hot with Green Chutney (see below).

Green Chutney

Grind together 1 cup fresh coriander, ½ cup fresh mint, 2-3 green chillies, black salt to taste, ¼ teaspoon sugar and 1 tablespoon lemon juice to a smooth paste using a little water if required.

Bhutta Seekh Kabab

8 ears of baby corn, slit lengthways into two
250 grams cottage cheese
5-6 green chillies, chopped
1 teaspoon ginger-garlic paste
3 tablespoons chopped fresh coriander
1 inch ginger, chopped
1 teaspoon Kashmiri chilli powder
1 tablespoon *garam masala* powder
2 teaspoons *chaat masala*
1 teaspoon *tandoori masala*
4 bread slices, soaked and crumbled
Salt to taste
Oil for shallow-frying

1. Blanch the ears of baby corn in two cups of water. Drain and cool.
2. Place the cottage cheese in a deep bowl and mash well. Add the green chillies, ginger-garlic paste, chopped coriander, ginger, chilli powder, *garam masala*, *chaat masala*, *tandoori masala*, bread and salt. Knead well to make a smooth dough.
3. Divide the dough into sixteen portions. Shape into elongated one-and-a-half-inch thick kabab. Insert a halved ear of baby corn into each kabab in such a way that two inches of the cob stick out.
4. Heat a non-stick *tawa*. Place the kabab on it, drizzle a little oil all around and shallow-fry till golden brown. Turn the kabab over frequently so that they brown evenly. Serve hot with ketchup.

Hare Matar Aur Paneer ke Shaami Kabab

½ cup shelled green peas, coarsely ground
350 grams cottage cheese
300 grams yam, boiled and mashed
1 tablespoon oil + for shallow-frying
1 teaspoon cumin seeds
1 inch ginger, chopped
6 green chillies, chopped
Salt to taste
2 tablespoons chopped fresh coriander
¼ teaspoon turmeric powder
1 teaspoon *garam masala* powder
1½ teaspoons red chilli powder
½ teaspoon *chaat masala*
½ teaspoon dried mango powder
2 tablespoons cornflour

1. Grate the cottage cheese and knead till smooth. Heat one tablespoon of oil in a non-stick pan. Add the cumin seeds and when they begin to change colour, add the green peas, ginger, green chillies and salt and sauté over medium heat for two minutes. Transfer to a plate and set aside to cool.
2. In a large bowl, combine the cottage cheese, sautéed green peas, yam, chopped coriander, turmeric powder, *garam masala* powder, chilli powder, *chaat masala*, dried mango powder and cornflour and mix well. Adjust the seasoning.
3. Divide the mixture into sixteen equal portions and shape into lemon-sized balls. Flatten the balls lightly to form kababs. Heat the oil in a non-stick frying pan and shallow-fry the kababs over medium heat till golden brown. Drain on absorbent paper. Serve hot with Green Chutney (page 7).

Rajma Galouti Kabab

1 cup red kidney beans
8 cashew nuts
1 tablespoon cudpahnut
¾ tablespoon poppy seeds
½ teaspoon caraway seeds
4 green cardamoms
3 black cardamoms
2 cloves
1 inch cinnamon
A generous pinch of saffron
¼ teaspoon screw pine essence
1 tablespoon pure ghee + for shallow-frying
½ inch ginger, chopped
5 garlic cloves, chopped
3 green chillies, chopped
2 tablespoons grated khoya/mawa
½ teaspoon white pepper powder
Salt to taste
½ tablespoon lemon juice
1 sprig fresh mint leaves
1 medium onion, cut into round slices

1. Soak the kidney beans in five cups of water preferably overnight. Boil in sufficient quantity of water until soft. Drain and set aside.
2. Dry-roast cashew nuts, cudpahnut and poppy seeds. Grind to a fine paste using a little water.

3. Dry-roast caraway seeds, green and black cardamoms, cloves and cinnamon. Cool and grind to a fine powder. Soak the saffron in the screw pine essence.
4. Heat one tablespoon ghee in a non-stick pan, add the ginger and garlic and sauté for a few seconds. Add the green chillies and sauté for one minute.
5. Add the kidney beans and cook for three to four minutes. Add the cashew nut paste and stir-fry for four to five minutes. Add khoya, white pepper powder and salt, stir-fry for four to five minutes.
6. Remove from heat. Cool and mash the kidney beans to a smooth paste. (In case the kidney bean paste is not firm, then cook paste further with addition of ghee till firm.)
7. Sprinkle powdered spices and soaked saffron. Adjust salt. Add lemon juice and mix thoroughly. Divide the mixture into equal portions and press them lightly.
8. Heat sufficient ghee in a non-stick frying pan and shallow-fry the patties until lightly coloured on both sides. Garnish with mint leaves and onion rings.
9. Serve with chutney of your choice.

Dahi Ke Kabab

½ cup drained (hung) yogurt
5 French beans, boiled and mashed
½ cup shelled green peas, boiled and mashed
9 small potatoes, boiled, peeled and mashed
2 tablespoons oil + for deep-frying
1 inch ginger, chopped
2 green chillies, chopped
1 teaspoon *garam masala* powder
1½ tablespoons chopped fresh coriander
Salt to taste
2½ tablespoons cornflour
1 cup breadcrumbs

1. Heat two tablespoons of the oil in non-stick pan on medium heat, add the ginger and green chillies, and sauté for a minute.
2. Add the French bean paste and green pea paste and sauté for two minutes.
3. Add the potatoes, *garam masala* powder, coriander and salt. Mix well, and set aside to cool.
4. Add the cornflour and mix well. Divide into eight equal portions and shape into balls.
5. Divide the drained yogurt into eight equal portions. Moisten the palms of your hands and place one portion of the potato mixture on them, and gently spread out into a small disc. Place one

portion of the yogurt in the centre, bring in the edges together and seal; ensuring that the yogurt is completely covered with the potato mixture. Roll into a ball and press lightly.

6. Roll the kababs in the breadcrumbs till they are covered all around.

7. Heat sufficient oil in a non-stick *kadai*. Add the kababs, a few at a time, and deep-fry on medium heat till they are evenly browned. Drain on an absorbent paper.

8. Serve hot with a chutney of your choice

Soya Shaami Kabab

1¼ cups soya *wadi*
4 cloves
1 inch cinnamon
1 bay leaf
1 teaspoon dried pomegranate seeds
1 tablespoon oil + for deep-frying
1 inch fresh ginger, peeled and grated
5 garlic cloves, peeled and chopped
4 dried red chillies, broken into two
2 green chillies, chopped
½ cup split Bengal gram
Salt to taste
1 cup breadcrumbs

1. Soak soya *wadi* in hot water for about twenty minutes. Squeeze out excess water.
2. Tie the cloves, cinnamon and bay leaf in a small piece of cloth to make a *potli*. Finely crush pomegranate seeds.
3. Heat one tablespoon of oil in a non-stick pan; add the spice *potli* and stir-fry for two minutes. Add the ginger, garlic, red chillies and green chillies, and continue to cook for another couple of minutes.

4. Add soya *wadi* and split Bengal gram and stir-fry for five minutes. Add one cup of water, mix, and lower heat. Cook until *dal* is cooked and dry.
5. Cool mixture thoroughly, discard *potli*, and grind mixture to a fine paste.
6. Add the pomegranate seeds, salt and breadcrumbs and knead into a stiff dough.
7. Divide into equal portions. Shape each portion into a round patty (*tikki*).
8. Heat the oil in a non-stick *kadai*. Deep-fry the patties in moderately hot oil until golden brown and crisp. Drain on absorbent paper.
9. Serve immediately with a spicy sauce.

Hara Bhara Kabab

200 grams fresh spinach leaves, blanched (see below) and chopped

¾ cup shelled green peas, boiled and mashed

3 potatoes, boiled and grated

2 green chillies, chopped

2 tablespoons chopped fresh coriander

1 inch ginger, chopped

1 teaspoon *chaat masala*

Salt to taste

2 tablespoons cornflour

2 tablespoons oil

1. Mix together the spinach, peas and potatoes. Add the green chillies, chopped coriander, ginger, *chaat masala* and salt. Mix in the cornflour.
2. Divide the mixture into twelve equal portions. Shape each portion into a ball and then press it between your palms to make a flat patty.
3. Heat a non-stick frying pan and pour one teaspoon of oil. Place six kababs keeping a little distance between each. Drizzle one teaspoon of oil all around the kababs and cook for two to three minutes or till the underside is golden brown.
4. Turn each over and drizzle one teaspoon oil all around and cook for two to three minutes more or till the other side is equally cooked to a golden brown. Drain on absorbent paper. Similarly cook the remaining six kababs. Drain on absorbent paper and serve hot.

Fruit Kabab

1 large apple, cut into 1½-inch pieces
1 large kiwi fruit, cut into 1½-inch pieces
2 large bananas, cut into 1½-inch pieces
2 pineapple slices, cut into 1½-inch pieces
5 plums, stoned and cut into 1½-inch pieces

Marinade

¼ cup honey
3 tablespoons lemon juice
3 tablespoons brown sugar
Salt to taste
2 tablespoons olive oil

1. For the marinade, mix together the honey, lemon juice, brown sugar, salt and olive oil.
2. Thread the fruit pieces onto skewers in the following order: apple, kiwi, banana, pineapple, plum. Pour the marinade over the fruit.
3. Heat a non-stick *tawa* on high heat and place the skewers over it and cook, rotating the skewers to cook the fruit evenly on all sides. Pour the remaining marinade over and cook till the fruits are cooked and golden. Serve hot with Pineapple Chutney (page 95)

Paneer Satay

500 grams cottage cheese, cut into 2-inch thick fingers
Salt to taste
2 tablespoons soy sauce
1 teaspoon lemon juice
4 garlic cloves, crushed
1 inch ginger, crushed
2 teaspoons brown sugar
2 teaspoons honey
Oil for basting

Peanut Sauce
1 tablespoon oil
1 small onion, chopped
½ inch ginger, crushed
4 garlic cloves, crushed
1 tablespoon soy sauce
6 tablespoons peanut butter
4 tablespoons Coconut Milk (see below)
1 tablespoon lemon juice
Salt to taste
1 tablespoon honey
1 fresh red chilli, seeded and chopped

1. Place the cottage cheese fingers in a bowl. Add the salt, soy sauce, lemon juice, garlic, ginger, brown sugar and honey, and mix. Marinate for one hour preferably in a refrigerator.
2. Soak satay sticks in water for at least fifteen minutes.
3. Heat the oil in a non-stick griddle or *tawa*. Thread the marinated cottage cheese onto satay sticks and place on the griddle. Pour some of the excess marinade over the cottage cheese and cook, turning the satay sticks to brown the cottage cheese evenly on all sides.
4. For the peanut sauce, heat the oil in a non-stick pan; add the onion and sauté for a few minutes.
5. Add the ginger and garlic, and continue to sauté. Add the soy sauce, peanut butter and two tablespoons of water. Stir in the coconut milk, lemon juice, salt and honey.
6. Add the chopped red chilli and remove from heat. Serve the satay with the sauce.

Coconut Milk

Process 1 cup grated fresh coconut in a blender with ¼ cup warm water. Pass the ground coconut through a piece of muslin or strainer pressing firmly to extract all the juice, or first milk. Add a ¼ cup of warm water to the strained coconut to get the second, thinner milk from the same solids.

Mushroom And Paneer Kabab

14-16 button mushrooms
200 grams cottage cheese, cut into 1½-inch cubes
18-20 cherry tomatoes
2 large capsicums, seeded and cut into 1-inch pieces
3 medium onions, cut into 1-inch pieces
2 inch ginger
8-10 garlic cloves
2-3 green chillies, seeded and roughly chopped
2 teaspoons oil
1 teaspoon red chilli flakes
2 teaspoons honey
1 teaspoon cumin powder
1 teaspoon *garam masala* powder
Salt to taste
2 teaspoons lemon juice
1 teaspoon *chaat masala*

1. Grind the ginger, garlic and green chillies to a paste. In a bowl, mix together the oil, ginger-garlic-green chilli paste, red chilli flakes, honey, cumin powder, *garam masala* powder, salt, lemon juice and *chaat masala*.
2. Marinate the cottage cheese, button mushrooms, cherry tomatoes, capsicums and onions in the mixture for about an hour. Take 8-inch long wooden satay sticks and soak them in water for half an hour. Remove from water and thread the marinated cottage cheese cubes, mushrooms, cherry tomatoes, capsicum and onion pieces one after the other onto the sticks.
3. Cook on an open charcoal fire or directly over gas flame for five minutes, rotating the stick for even cooking. Alternately, cook in a preheated oven for about fifteen minutes. Serve hot.

Khatte Meethe Vegetable Seekh

½ medium potato, boiled, peeled and mashed
½ medium carrot, boiled and chopped
¼ cup shelled green peas, boiled and mashed
150 grams cottage cheese, grated
1 teaspoon ginger paste
½ teaspoon dried mango powder
1 teaspoon *chaat masala*
½ teaspoon red chilli powder
1 green chilli, chopped
1 tablespoon chopped fresh coriander
1½ tablespoons mango chutney
1 tablespoon butter
2 tablespoons roasted split Bengal gram powder
Salt to taste
Oil for shallow-frying

1. Combine the potato, carrot, peas, cottage cheese, ginger paste, dried mango powder, *chaat masala*, chilli powder, green chilli, chopped coriander, mango chutney, butter, roasted split Bengal gram powder and salt to taste in a bowl.
2. Divide mixture into sixteen equal portions. Press each portion into a cylindrical shape around a skewer. Heat a non-stick *tawa*; add a little oil and place the skewers on it.
3. Cook, rotating the skewers from time to time, to cook the kabab evenly on all sides till golden brown. Serve hot with a chutney of your choice.

Raunaq-E-Seekh

3 medium carrots, peeled and grated
12 thin long beans, strings removed and chopped
125 grams cauliflower, grated
1 medium green capsicum, chopped
1 cup green peas, blanched and mashed
100 grams American corn, blanched and mashed
3 medium potatoes, boiled, peeled and mashed
6 tablespoons oil
1 teaspoon caraway seeds
6 green chillies, minced
1 tablespoon ginger paste
1 tablespoon garlic paste
1 teaspoon *garam masala* powder
1 teaspoon salt
1 teaspoon white pepper powder
4 tablespoons roasted split Bengal gram powder
2 teaspoons lemon juice
2 teaspoons *chaat masala*

1. Soak wooden skewers (satay sticks) in water for at least fifteen minutes.
2. Place a non-stick *kadai* on medium heat and pour in three tablespoons oil; add the caraway seeds. Sauté for ten seconds. Add the chillies, ginger paste, garlic paste and sauté for thirty seconds.

3. Add the carrots, beans, cauliflower and capsicum and cook for eight to ten minutes or till all the moisture evaporates.
4. Add the green peas, American corn and potatoes and stir well. Add the *garam masala* powder, salt and white pepper powder and stir.
5. Add the roasted gram powder and lemon juice and stir. Take the pan off the heat. Allow it to cool completely.
6. Divide the vegetable mixture into eight portions. Take a portion of the vegetable mixture and pat onto a satay stick in a cylindrical or sausage shape. Make the remaining *seekh* similarly.
7. Place a non-stick grill pan on medium heat. Place the *seekh*, two at a time, and cook for five to six minutes, turning the sticks a few times so that the *seekh* get evenly cooked all around to a light golden brown.
8. Slide the *seekh* off the satay sticks and place them on serving plate. Slice them into two pieces diagonally. Sprinkle *chaat masala* over and serve hot.

Vegetable Seekh Kabab

1 medium potato, boiled and mashed
1 medium carrot, grated
½ cup green peas, crushed
5-6 French beans, finely chopped
1 teaspoon ginger paste
1 teaspoon dried mango powder
2 teaspoons *chaat masala*
3-4 green chillies, chopped
1½ tablespoons *chhunda*
3 tablespoons roasted split Bengal gram powder
150 grams cottage cheese, grated
Salt to taste

1. Heat a non-stick *kadai*. Add the ginger paste and cook for half a minute. Add the mashed potato, carrot, green peas and French beans and roast till fragrant.
2. Add the dried mango powder, *chaat masala*, green chillies, *chhunda*, roasted split Bengal powder and continue to cook for two to three minutes. Add the cottage cheese and mix well. Add the salt and mix again.
3. Divide into eight equal portions. Take each portion and spread it around a skewer in a cylindrical shape. Heat a non-stick *tawa* and place the skewers on it. Cook on medium heat, rotating the skewers from time to time so that the kababs gets cooked evenly from all sides, to a golden brown. Serve hot with chutney of your choice.

Phal-Subz Seekh

2 large unripe bananas
2 medium potatoes, boiled and mashed
200 grams fresh button mushrooms, chopped
1 small carrot, grated
4 broccoli florets, chopped
1½ tablespoons butter + 4 tablespoons for basting
¾ teaspoon carom seeds
¾ tablespoon chopped fresh coriander
¾ inch ginger, chopped
1½ fresh red chillies, chopped
Salt to taste
8 prunes, stoned and chopped
½ teaspoon black salt
¾ teaspoon black pepper powder
½ teaspoon green cardamom powder
A pinch of edible sandalwood powder
A pinch of dried rose petal powder
½ cup breadcrumbs
1½ tablespoons oil

1. Boil, cool, peel and grate the bananas.
2. Heat one and a half tablespoons of butter in a non-stick pan; add the carom seeds and sauté over medium heat for ten seconds.
3. Add the mushrooms, carrots and broccoli, and sauté till the moisture evaporates. Add the chopped coriander, ginger, red chillies and salt.

4. Stir and remove from heat and set aside to cool.
5. Place the cooled mixture in a blender with the grated bananas, potatoes, prunes, black salt, pepper powder, cardamom powder, sandalwood powder, rose petal powder, and breadcrumbs and process till smooth.
6. Transfer the mixture to a bowl and divide into six equal portions. Pat the mixture onto skewers into four-inch long *seekh* kababs.
7. Preheat the oven to 180°C/350°F/Gas Mark 4.
8. Arrange the satay sticks on a greased tray, brush with butter and cook in a preheated oven for 6-7 minutes.
9. Gently slide the kababs from the satay sticks onto a plate. Cut each into four pieces and serve immediately.

Smoky Fish Kabab

1 (300-400 grams) fish (pomfret/king fish), cut into fillets
2 medium tomatoes, seeded and cut into 1-inch cubes
16 shallots
16 stuffed olives
2 tablespoons oil

Marinade
3 tablespoons lemon juice
1 teaspoon crushed peppercorns
Salt to taste
1 tablespoon ginger paste
2 tablespoons brown sugar

1. Wash fish fillets and cut into one-inch sized cubes.
2. Mix together the lemon juice, crushed pepper, salt, ginger paste and brown sugar. Marinate the fish, tomato and baby onions in this for an hour.
3. Skewer onto a toothpick or satay stick the marinated cubes in this order: fish cube, baby onion, stuffed olive and tomato cube. Arrange the toothpicks on a wire rack and cook on Grill TOP and BOTTOM for eight minutes.
4. Baste with oil and cook on Grill TOP and BOTTOM for four minutes. Serve immediately.

Oriental Fish Kabab

Kabab

500 grams fish fillet, cut into 24 cubes
1 tablespoon lemon juice
16 button mushrooms, stemmed
24 seedless black grapes
12 lychees, peeled, halved and seeded
½ tablespoon oil

Sauce

1 tablespoon oil
1 inch ginger, finely chopped
2 garlic cloves, crushed
2 tablespoons soy sauce
1 teaspoon peppercorn, crushed
2 tablespoon red wine (optional)
2 teaspoons honey

1. Apply lemon juice to the fish cubes and set aside to marinate.
2. Cook the mushrooms in a non-stick pan on medium heat with a lid on for three to four minutes. Toss them occasionally. Remove, strain and set aside and reserve the cooking liquid for the sauce.
3. Heat the oil in a small non-stick pan over moderate heat, add the garlic and ginger to the pan and cook for fifteen seconds on medium heat. Add the soy sauce, peppercorn, reserved cooking liquid, red wine, one-fourth cup of water and bring to boil. Add the honey and mix well.

4. Lower the heat and simmer gently for two to three minutes. Remove and keep warm till the kababs are ready.
5. Thread the fish, cooked mushrooms, black grapes and lychee halves onto the wooden skewers.
6. Brush with the oil and grill for ten minutes, alternatively cook it in a preheated oven at 180°C/350°F/Gas Mark 4 for ten to twelve or until the fish is tender. You can also cook this dish on a griddle plate or a thick non-stick pan. Make sure to turn the skewers at regular intervals for even cooking.
7. Lace the kababs with the sauce and serve immediately.

Jalpari Kabab

8 fish fillets
½ cup shrimps
8 medium prawns
Butter for basting

First Marinade

½ inch ginger
5 garlic cloves
1 cup drained (hung) yogurt
½ cup fresh cream
1 teaspoon carom seeds
1 egg
1 teaspoon *garam masala* powder
1 tablespoon lemon juice
1 tablespoon oil
Salt to taste

Second Marinade

½ inch ginger
5 garlic cloves
¾ cup drained (hung) curd
1 teaspoon red chilli powder
¼ teaspoon turmeric powder
1 teaspoon carom seed
1 egg
½ cup fresh cream
¼ teaspoon *garam masala* powder
1 teaspoon lemon juice
1 tbsp oil
Salt to taste
½ cup grated cheese

1. Trim, wash, pat dry and flatten fish fillets using a steak hammer. Shell, devein and wash shrimps thoroughly. Shell prawns leaving the tails intact, devein and wash thoroughly. Squeeze the shrimps and prawns between the palm of your hands to remove excess moisture.
2. For the first marinade, peel, grind together the ginger and garlic into a fine paste. Mix with rest of the ingredients. Apply this marinade on both sides of the fish fillets and allow to stand for half an hour.
3. Mix all the ingredients for the second marinade, divide into two portions and marinate prawns and shrimps in one portion each for half an hour.
4. Preheat an oven to 240^0C/475^0F/Gas Mark 9.
5. To prepare the kababs, place two marinated shrimps and a prawn at the centre of the marinated fish fillet leaving the tail of the prawn on the outer edge. Roll and secure with a toothpick.
6. Arrange on skewers and cook in a *tandoor* for eight to ten minutes, basting occasionally with butter, or cook in the preheated oven for ten to twelve minutes basting occasionally with butter.
7. Serve hot with Mint Chutney (page 95).

Murgh Neza Kabab

700 grams chicken legs
2 tablespoons ginger paste
2 tablespoons garlic paste
2 teaspoons salt
½ teaspoon white pepper powder
½ teaspoon *garam masala* powder
¼ teaspoon crushed dried fenugreek leaves
3 teaspoons vinegar
2 tablespoons chopped fresh coriander
½ teaspoon green cardamom powder
3 tablespoons oil
1 cup gram flour
1 egg
4 tablespoons cream
2 tablespoons melted butter
1 lemon, cut into wedges
1 large onion, cut into rings
1 large tomato, cut into slices

1. Loosen the thigh-bone from the flesh of the chicken legs but do not remove it fully.
2. Combine together the ginger paste, garlic paste, salt, white pepper powder, *garam masala* powder, dried fenugreek leaves, vinegar, chopped coriander and cardamom powder in a deep bowl. Add the chicken legs and mix well so that all the legs are well coated with the marinade. Marinate for twenty minutes.

3. Heat the oil in a medium-sized non-stick frying pan on medium heat. When small bubbles appear at the bottom of the pan, reduce the heat to low, add the gram flour and sauté till fragrant and lightly coloured. Transfer the contents to a bowl. Let it cool.
4. Break the egg and add it to the gram flour. Whisk to make a smooth paste. Add the cream and whisk again.
5. Coat the chicken legs with the paste and set aside for twenty minutes.
6. Preheat the oven to 200°C/400°F/Gas Mark 6.
7. Thread the chicken legs first along the bone and again through the thigh onto the skewers. Cook in the preheated oven for seven to eight minutes. Take the skewers out and baste each leg with half tablespoon of melted butter. Place the skewers back in the oven and cook for seven to eight minutes more or till lightly coloured.
8. Remove from skewers onto a serving dish, garnish with lemon wedges, onion rings and tomato slices and serve hot.

Nawabi Kalmi Kabab

400 grams boneless chicken, cut into 2-inch cubes

1 inch cinnamon

½ teaspoon caraway seeds

2 cloves

8-10 saffron threads

1 teaspoon ginger paste

1 teaspoon garlic paste

½ cup yogurt

2 tablespoons lemon juice

1 egg, whisked

¼ cup refined flour

¾ teaspoon salt

1 large onion, cut into rings

A few sprigs of fresh mint leaves, chopped

1 lemon, cut into wedges

Butter for basting

1. Wash the chicken pieces and wipe them dry. Prick each piece with a fork in two to three places.
2. Place a small non-stick frying pan on medium heat, add the cinnamon, caraway seeds, cloves and saffron and dry-roast lightly. Cool and grind to a fine powder.

3. Combine the ginger paste, garlic paste, yogurt, roasted spice powder, lemon juice, egg, flour and salt in a deep bowl.
4. Add the chicken pieces and toss so that all the chicken pieces are well coated with the *masala*. Cover the bowl with cling film and place it in a refrigerator to marinate for two to three hours.
5. Preheat an oven to 200°C/400°F/Gas Mark 6.
6. Arrange the chicken pieces on a baking tray and bake for eight minutes. Baste with butter and bake for two minutes more.
7. You can also grill it in the griller. Place the marinated chicken on a drip-tray and grill till golden brown. For best results cook in a hot *tandoor*.
8. Serve hot, garnished with onion rings, mint leaves and lemon wedges.

Kabab Kombdyache

4 (100 grams each) boneless chicken breasts
Salt to taste
2 tablespoons oil
4 medium onions, sliced
10 black peppercorns
1 tablespoon coriander seeds
1 inch cinnamon
3-4 cloves
3-4 green cardamoms
1 cup drained (hung) yogurt
1 tablespoon ginger paste
¼ cup cream
A pinch of crushed black peppercorns
2 tablespoons oil
1 tablespoon lemon juice

1. Soak satay sticks in water for at least fifteen minutes.
2. Clean, wash and cut chicken breasts into three lengthways. Mix in salt and set aside.
3. Heat the oil in a non-stick *kadai* and sauté the onions till brown. Cool and grind onions to a fine paste.
4. Dry-roast peppercorns, coriander seeds, cinnamon, cloves and cardamoms. Grind the roasted spices to a fine powder.

5. Combine the browned onion paste, roasted spice powder, drained yogurt, ginger paste, cream and salt. Add the chicken and set aside to marinate for two hours, preferably in a refrigerator.
6. Thread the chicken pieces onto the satay sticks and sprinkle crushed black peppercorns over the chicken.
7. Arrange the sticks on the barbecue or grill and cook, basting with oil every now and then and turning the sticks so that the chicken cooks evenly on all sides. Sprinkle with lemon juice.
8. Alternatively, place the sticks on a greased non-stick *tawa* and cook over a gas flame till done. Sprinkle with lemon juice, cover and cook till tender.
9. Transfer to a serving plate and serve hot.

Chicken Gilafi Seekh Kabab

½ kg minced chicken
2 large onions, sliced
Oil for deep-frying
1½ inches ginger
10 garlic cloves
15-20 fresh mint leaves
A few sprigs of fresh coriander, finely chopped
2-3 green chillies, finely chopped
1 teaspoon red chilli powder
1 teaspoon *garam masala* powder
1 teaspoon lemon juice
Salt to taste
1 tablespoon cashew nut powder
10-12 cashew nuts, coarsely powdered
1 egg, beaten
Butter, for basting
Lemon wedges, for garnishing

1. Wash the chicken and press between the palms of your hand to remove excess water.
2. Heat sufficient oil in a non-stick *kadai* and deep-fry the onions until golden brown in colour. Drain on an absorbent paper and set aside.
3. Grind together the ginger and garlic to a fine paste. Chop finely the mint leaves, reserving a few for garnishing.

4. In a large bowl, combine the chicken, browned onions, chopped coriander, mint leaves, ginger-garlic paste, chopped green chillies, chilli powder, *garam masala* powder, lemon juice and salt.
5. Process the above mixture in a blender for half a minute. Transfer the mixture to a bowl and add cashew nut powder. Mix well, cover and allow it to stand for half an hour preferably in a refrigerator. Mix together the coarsely ground cashew nuts and beaten egg, and set aside.
6. Preheat an oven at 240°C/475°F/Gas Mark 9 or light a *tandoor*.
7. Divide the mince mixture into twenty equal portions. Moisten the hands and dab portions of the mince mixture onto skewers in a cylindrical shape, three inches long and leaving a gap of one inch between each kabab.
8. Cook in a preheated oven for twelve to fifteen or in the *tandoor* for eight to ten minutes till half done. Brush it with the egg-cashew nut mixture and cook till done, basting it with butter occasionally. Serve hot, garnished with lemon wedges and reserved mint leaves.

Note: It is important that the kababs are juicy and moist; otherwise it would taste very dry. Do not overcook.

Chicken Makhmali Kabab

4 (200 grams each) chicken breasts
4-6 green chillies, chopped
1 inch ginger, roughly chopped
5-6 garlic cloves, roughly chopped
⅔ cup drained (hung) yogurt
¼ cup grated processed cheese
¼ cup fresh cream
½ teaspoon nutmeg powder
2 teaspoons *garam masala* powder
1 tablespoon honey
½ tablespoon lemon juice
Salt to taste
¼ cup butter

1. Remove the skin and bone and cut each chicken breast into two. Grind together the green chillies, ginger and garlic into a smooth paste. Rub the paste into the chicken, cover and set aside for fifteen minutes.
2. In a bowl, whisk together the drained yogurt, cheese, cream, nutmeg powder, *garam masala* powder, honey, lemon juice and salt to taste. Marinate chicken in this mixture for three hours in a refrigerator. Place chicken pieces, an inch apart, on a wire rack.
3. Cook chicken in a Grill TOP and BOTTOM for twenty minutes, brushing with butter every five minutes. Serve hot with Green Chutney (page 7).

Chef's Tip: Use supremes of chicken for tender succulent kababs.

Pankhari Kabab

16 chicken wings and shoulder

First Marinade

1 tablespoon ginger-garlic paste

Salt to taste

2 teaspoons white pepper powder

Second Marinade

100 grams processed cheese, grated

1 egg white

200 ml cream

1 tablespoon ginger-garlic paste

Salt to taste

2 teaspoons white pepper powder

1 teaspoon cinnamon powder

4 green chillies, chopped

2 tablespoons melted butter

1. Cut and clean the chicken wings and shoulder. Wash, pat dry and set aside.
2. For the first marinade, mix together the ginger-garlic paste, salt and white pepper powder in a bowl. Rub the mixture into the chicken wings and shoulder and marinate for one hour in a refrigerator.

3. For the second marinade, place the cheese in a tray; add the egg white and rub it in with your palm in one direction. Add the cream gradually so that it blends well.
4. Add the ginger-garlic paste, salt, pepper powder, cinnamon powder, green chillies and melted butter one after the other, and mix well.
5. Coat the chicken wings and shoulder with the marinade and set aside for one or two hours in the refrigerator.
6. Preheat the oven to 200°C/400°F/Gas Mark 6.
7. Thread the marinated chicken wings and shoulder one inch apart onto skewer.
8. Cook in the preheated oven for fifteen minutes or in a moderately hot *tandoor* or over a charcoal grill for four to six minutes. Remove and suspend the skewers so that the excess moisture drains off completely.
9. Baste with melted butter and roast for four to five minutes longer. Serve hot with any salad and Green Chutney (page 7).

Chicken Seekh Kabab

500 grams finely minced chicken
1-2 green chillies, finely chopped
1 medium onion, finely chopped
1 inch ginger, finely chopped
4 garlic cloves, finely chopped
2 tablespoons finely chopped cashew nuts
1 teaspoon *chaat masala*
1 teaspoon *garam masala* powder
1 teaspoon white pepper powder
2 tablespoons chopped fresh coriander
1 tablespoon lemon juice
Salt to taste
Oil, as required
2 tablespoons butter

1. In a bowl, mix together the minced chicken, green chillies, onion, ginger, garlic, cashew nuts, *chaat masala*, *garam masala* powder, white pepper powder, chopped coriander, lemon juice and salt.
2. Alternatively, you can use boneless chicken and grind it together with the green chillies, onion, ginger and garlic. Add the remaining ingredients and mix.
3. Heat a non-stick *tawa* and drizzle some oil on it. Wet your hands, take a little chicken mixture and shape it around a satay stick, pressing the mixture firmly.
4. Place the *seekh* kababs on the *tawa*. Cook, turning from time to time, so that the kababs cook evenly all around. Baste with butter at regular intervals. Serve hot.

Chef's Tip: For best results, use minced chicken breast.

Kombdi Pulava Kabab

4 (150 grams each) boneless chicken breasts
1 tablespoon coriander seeds
2 green cardamoms
½ inch cinnamon
2 cloves
1 large onion
⅛ cup almonds, blanched and ground
¼ cup yogurt
¼ tablespoon black peppercorns, crushed
½ tablespoon ginger paste
¼ tablespoon garlic paste
Salt to taste
Black salt to taste
Ghee for shallow-frying
2 lemons, cut into wedges

1. Soak satay sticks in water for at least fifteen minutes.
2. Preheat the oven to 180°C/350°F/Gas Mark 4.
3. Heat a non-stick *tawa* and dry-roast coriander seeds, cardamoms, cinnamon and cloves, separately. Grind the spices to a powder.
4. Slit the chicken breasts into two and then into strips. Thread them onto the wooden skewers.

5. Roast the onion in the oven for thirty to forty minutes.
6. Combine the roasted onion, ground almonds, yogurt, crushed peppercorns, ginger paste, garlic paste, salt and black salt. Add the roasted spice powder and mix well.
7. Add the mixture to the skewered chicken and set aside to marinate for half an hour.
8. Heat some ghee on a non-stick *tawa* till very hot. Place the chicken on it and cook on high heat for two minutes. Lower heat and cook, turning the skewers a couple of times, till the kababs are golden brown on both sides. Drizzle a little more ghee over the kababs if necessary.
9. Alternatively, cook the chicken in a preheated oven or *tandoor*. Serve hot with lemon wedges.

Dahi Murgh Kabab

600 grams minced chicken
¼ cup split Bengal gram
2 tablespoons oil + for deep-frying
1 teaspoon cumin seeds
1 teaspoon coriander seeds
5-6 black peppercorns
2 black cardamoms
1½ inches ginger, chopped
10 garlic cloves, chopped
Salt to taste
2 teaspoons red chilli powder
½ teaspoon green cardamom powder
A pinch of mace powder
½ teaspoon *garam masala* powder
2 eggs, beaten

Stuffing

¼ cup drained (hung) yogurt
1 small onion, finely chopped
2 teaspoons chopped fresh mint
Salt to taste

1. Soak the split Bengal gram in two cups of water for at least three hours. Drain.
2. For the stuffing, squeeze the chopped onion between your palms to remove excess water. In a bowl, mix the drained yogurt, chopped onion, mint and salt. Divide into sixteen equal portions, cover and place in a refrigerator.

3. Heat two tablespoons of oil in a non-stick pan; add the cumin seeds, coriander seeds, peppercorns, cardamom seeds, ginger and garlic, and stir-fry for one minute over a moderate heat. Add the minced chicken and sauté for five minutes.
4. Add the soaked split Bengal gram, salt, chilli powder, cardamom powder, mace powder and *garam masala* powder. Stir well for two minutes.
5. Add one and a half cups of water and bring the mixture to a boil. Lower the heat and cook, covered, till the split Bengal gram is completely cooked. Cook over a high heat to dry out the mixture completely, stirring continuously. Remove from the heat and set aside to cool.
6. Grind the chicken and the gram mixture till smooth. Check the seasoning.
7. Divide the chicken mixture into sixteen equal portions. Flatten each portion in the palm of your hand and place a portion of onion and yogurt stuffing in the centre. Shape into round patties and flatten slightly.
8. Heat the oil in a non-stick *kadai*. Dip each *tikki* in the beaten egg and deep-fry till golden brown. Drain on absorbent paper. Serve hot with onion rings and Mint Chutney (page 95).

Chef's Tip: If the chicken mixture is still too moist after cooking, add some roasted gram flour or powdered roasted split Bengal gram.

Potli Kabab

4 (115 grams each) boneless chicken breasts
250 grams minced chicken
2 tablespoons ginger-garlic paste
2 tablespoons chopped fresh coriander
5-8 fresh mint leaves, chopped
2 green chillies, chopped
Salt to taste
½ cup drained (hung) yogurt
2 tablespoons gram flour
2 tablespoons cream
1 teaspoon green chilli paste
½ teaspoon *garam masala* powder
Melted butter for basting

1. Slit the chicken breasts without cutting through. Open them out. Flatten slightly with a steak hammer or with the back of a knife.
2. Marinate the minced chicken in a mixture of one tablespoon ginger-garlic paste, the fresh coriander, fresh mint, green chillies and salt for about fifteen minutes.
3. Divide the chicken mixture into four equal portions and shape them into balls. Place each ball on a flattened chicken breast. Shape the chicken breast around the ball to cover it completely. Seal the edges with a tooth pick.

4. Put the yogurt into a bowl; and add the gram flour, remaining ginger-garlic paste, salt, cream, green chilli paste and *garam masala* powder and mix well.
5. Marinate the stuffed chicken balls in this mixture for two hours preferably in a refrigerator.
6. Preheat an oven to 200°C/400°F/Gas Mark 6.
7. Place the balls sealed end facing down on a greased baking tray keeping a distance of an inch between each ball.
8. Cook in the preheated oven for twenty minutes basting with the melted butter a few times in between.
9. Transfer to a plate. Serve hot with a salad and chutney of your choice.

Chef's Tip: If the minced chicken is not very fine, grind a couple of times in a food processor.

Mulayam Murgh Seekh

500 grams minced chicken breast
¼ cup fresh coriander, finely chopped
2-3 green chillies, roughly chopped
1 inch ginger, roughly chopped
4-6 cloves garlic, roughly chopped
8-10 cashew nuts
2 egg yolks
Salt to taste
1 teaspoon *garam masala* powder
1 teaspoon white pepper powder
2 tablespoons butter
1 tablespoon lemon juice
1 teaspoon *chaat masala*

1. Grind together the chopped coriander, green chillies, ginger and garlic to a fine paste without adding any water.
2. Soak the cashew nuts in warm water for ten minutes; drain and grind to a fine paste.
3. Blend the ginger, garlic, coriander-green chilli paste with cashew nut paste and egg yolks. Add the mixture to the minced chicken with salt, *garam masala* powder and white pepper powder. Mix thoroughly and set aside, preferably in the refrigerator, for at least half an hour.

(image on page 58)

4. Divide the chicken mixture into ten to twelve equal portions. Moisten your palm and shape each portion along a skewer into four to five-inch long kababs.
5. Cook in a moderately hot *tandoor* for about eight to ten minutes turning occasionally.
6. Brush the cooked kababs with butter and cook again for a minute in the *tandoor*.
7. The kababs can also be cooked in a preheated oven at 220°C/425°F/Gas Mark 7 for about ten minutes. Brush the kababs with butter and cook for two minutes more.
8. Sprinkle lemon juice and *chaat masala* on the cooked kababs and serve hot.

Caribbean Chicken Kabab

4 (200 grams each) boneless chicken breasts, cut into 1-inch pieces
2 medium onions
5-6 dried red chillies, seeded
8-10 garlic cloves
2-3 sprigs of fresh parsley
7-8 basil leaves
½ tablespoon lemon juice
1 tablespoon Worcestershire sauce
5-6 peppercorns
½ teaspoon curry powder
Salt to taste
1 medium capsicum, seeded and cut into 1-inch cubes
2 tinned pineapple slices, cut into 1-inch cubes
1 medium tomato, seeded and cut into 1-inch cubes

1. Chop one onion and cut the other into one-and-half-inch cubes..
2. Grind together the dried chillies, chopped onion, garlic, parsley, basil, lemon juice, Worcestershire sauce, peppercorns, curry powder and salt to make a coarse paste. Transfer the paste to a bowl and add the chicken.
3. Add the capsicum, pineapple, tomato and onion cubes and let them marinate for two hours, preferably in a refrigerator. Thread the chicken, capsicum, pineapple, tomato and onion cubes one after the other onto skewers. Reserve the remaining marinade for basting.
4. Heat a non-stick *tawa*. Place the skewers on the *tawa* and cook, basting with reserved marinade every five minutes, for ten to twelve minutes or until chicken is done. Serve hot.

Chicken Satay

4 medium boneless chicken breasts, skin removed
2 tablespoons lemon juice
1 tablespoon dark soy sauce
1 teaspoon oil
1 teaspoon red chilli powder
Salt to taste

Peanut Sauce

¼ cup roasted peanuts, crushed coarsely
1 small onion, grated
4 garlic cloves, chopped
1 teaspoon oil
½ teaspoon red chilli powder
1 tablespoon dark soy sauce
3 tablespoons tomato purée
2 teaspoons honey
Salt to taste

1. Cut each chicken breast into half-inch broad strips. Flatten the strips lightly.
2. Mix together the lemon juice, soy sauce, oil and chilli powder in a bowl. Add the chicken and set aside to marinate for one hour.
3. Thread the chicken onto the wooden skewers.

4. Heat a non-stick flat *tawa*, grease it lightly with a few drops of oil and place a few skewers with the chicken on it. Cook on high heat, turning frequently, for three to four minutes, or till just cooked.
5. Alternately, cook on a preheated grill for ten to twelve minutes or until done, turning skewers a couple of times.
6. For the peanut sauce, heat the oil in a non-stick pan; add the grated onion and chopped garlic. Cook on high heat, stirring continuously, for half a minute.
7. Add chilli powder and stir in dark soy sauce, tomato purée, honey, crushed peanuts, salt and one cup of water.
8. Bring the sauce to a boil and simmer for five minutes, stirring occasionally.
9. Serve chicken satay with peanut sauce.

Chef's Tip: Soak wooden skewers in water for half an hour prior to cooking, to prevent them from burning while cooking. This is particularly necessary while grilling or cooking over an open flame.

Khaas Seekh

8 satay sticks
½ cup grated cottage cheese
1½ teaspoons green cardamom powder
1 tablespoon *garam masala* powder
1 tablespoon chopped fresh mint leaves
600 grams minced chicken
1 egg
1½ teaspoons salt
1 teaspoon white pepper powder
2 green chillies, chopped
2 tablespoons oil

1. Soak the satay sticks in two cups of water for thirty minutes. Drain and to dry.
2. Place the cottage cheese, three-fourth teaspoon cardamom powder, half tablespoon *garam masala* powder and mint leaves in a deep bowl. Mix, mashing well using your hands. Divide into eight equal portions. Take a portion of the mixture and place on a satay stick and press it around the stick in a thin layer. Press the ends firmly.
3. Place the minced chicken in another bowl. Break the egg and add to the chicken. Add the salt, remaining cardamom powder, pepper powder, the remaining *garam masala* powder and green chillies and mix well. Divide into eight equal portions.

4. Take a portion of the mixture and spread it over the cottage cheese mixture. You can keep the *seekh* in the refrigerator for one hour before cooking.
5. Heat two tablespoons of oil in a shallow non-stick frying pan on medium heat. Place the *seekh* in the pan and cook, turning the *seekh* continuously so that they are evenly cooked and golden brown all around.
6. Transfer onto an absorbent paper. When slightly cooled, gently slide the *seekh* from the satay sticks and place them on a serving plate and serve immediately.

Kastoori Kabab

500 grams minced chicken
1½ tablespoons ginger-garlic paste
1½ tablespoons lemon juice
Salt to taste
A few saffron threads
1 tablespoon milk
2 tablespoons butter
6 tablespoons gram flour
5 tablespoons breadcrumbs
1 teaspoon white pepper powder
1 teaspoon green cardamom powder
4 tablespoons chopped fresh coriander
½ teaspoon red chilli powder
2 eggs, beaten
½ teaspoon caraway seeds
Oil for shallow-frying
1 teaspoon *chaat masala*

1. Marinate the minced chicken in a mixture of ginger-garlic paste, lemon juice and salt for fifteen minutes. Soak the saffron in the milk. Heat one tablespoon of butter in a non-stick pan; add the gram flour and sauté over a medium heat till golden brown and fragrant. Set aside three teaspoons of the roasted gram flour.
2. To the remaining gram flour add the breadcrumbs, white pepper powder, cardamom powder, chopped coriander, salt and chilli powder. Add this to the marinated mince mixture and shape into patties (*tikki*). Mix together the eggs, caraway seeds, salt, saffron-flavoured milk and the reserved roasted gram flour.
3. Heat sufficient oil in a non-stick pan. Dip the patties in the egg batter and shallow-fry till golden brown. Sprinkle the *chaat masala* and serve hot with Green Chutney (page 7).

Tangdi Kabab

Chicken drumsticks

8 (500 grams) chicken drumsticks with bone
½ tablespoon lemon juice
1 cup drained (hung) yogurt
2 tablespoons gram flour
2 teaspoons ginger paste
2 teaspoons garlic paste
1 teaspoon turmeric powder
1 teaspoon *garam masala* powder
1 teaspoon red chilli powder
½ teaspoon salt
4 green chillies, chopped
2 tablespoons melted butter, for basting
1 teaspoon *chaat masala*
1 lemon, cut into wedges

1. Clean and trim off excess fat and skin from the drumsticks.
2. Wash well and dry them with an absorbent kitchen towel. Make three to four long deep incisions on each drumstick. Apply the lemon juice and set aside for thirty minutes, preferably in the refrigerator.
3. Place a medium non-stick pan on low heat. Add the gram flour and roast over low heat, stirring continuously, for four to five minutes or till light brown and fragrant.

4. Allow it to cool and transfer into a deep bowl. Add the drained yogurt, ginger paste, garlic paste, turmeric powder, *garam masala* powder, chilli powder, half teaspoon salt and chillies.
5. Add the chicken drumsticks to this mixture and mix well so that the drumsticks are well and evenly coated. Cover the bowl and place in the refrigerator to marinate for one to two hours.
6. Preheat an oven to 220°C/425°F/Gas Mark 7.
7. Pierce metal skewers through the marinated chicken drumsticks. Bake in the preheated oven for five minutes.
8. Lower the oven temperature to 200°C/400°F/Gas Mark 6 and bake for fifteen to twenty minutes more. After each five minutes, baste the drumsticks with butter and rotate them to ensure even cooking and colour.
9. Take the drumsticks out from the oven and gently remove from skewers. Sprinkle with *chaat masala* and garnish with lemon wedges. Serve immediately.

Shikampuri Kabab

250 grams minced mutton
8 teaspoons oil +for deep-frying
1½ medium onions, sliced
2 tablespoons pure ghee
½ teaspoon caraway seeds
2 dried red chillies, broken
½ inch ginger, roughly chopped
5 garlic cloves, roughly chopped
1 tablespoon split Bengal gram, soaked for ½ hour
5 tablespoons fresh mint leaves
5 tablespoons chopped fresh coriander
½ tablespoon lemon juice
1 teaspoon salt
1 egg, beaten

Stuffing

1 cup yogurt
1 green chilli, chopped
1 large onion, chopped
2 tablespoons chopped fresh mint leaves
½ teaspoon salt
½ teaspoon roasted cumin seeds

1. Wash the ground mutton under running water and drain well in a colander.
2. Heat sufficient oil in a non-stick *kadai*; add the onions and deep-fry, till the onions are well browned. Drain on an absorbent paper.
3. Place a non-stick pan on medium heat and pour in the ghee; add the caraway seeds, red chillies, ginger and garlic and sauté for one minute. Add the minced mutton and sauté for five minutes, stirring occasionally.
4. Drain the split Bengal gram and add to the pan. Stir and sauté for one minute. Add the mint leaves and chopped coriander and stir well.
5. Cook for five minutes. Remove from heat and set aside to cool.
6. Transfer the cooled mixture into a blender jar. Add the browned onions, lemon juice and salt and blend to a coarse paste.
7. Transfer the paste into a bowl. Divide the ground mutton mixture into eight equal portions.
8. For the stuffing, tie the yogurt in a piece of muslin and hang for an hour till most of the moisture has drained away.

9. Transfer into a bowl, add the chilli, onion, mint leaves, salt and roasted cumin seeds to the yogurt. Mix well and divide into eight equal portions.
10. Flatten one portion of the ground mutton mixture in the palm of your hand and place a portion of yogurt stuffing in the centre. Gather the edges, shape into a round discl and flatten slightly
11. Place a non-stick frying pan on medium heat and pour in 2 teaspoons of oil. Dip two kababs in the beaten egg and place them in the frying pan and cook, turning sides once, for three to four minutes or till both the sides are cooked and lightly browned.
12. Drain on an absorbent paper. Cook the remaining kababs similarly. Serve hot with onion rings and Green Chutney (page 7).

Patther Kabab

800 grams boneless mutton, cut into 1½-inch pieces
2 inches ginger
10 garlic cloves
5 green chillies
3 inches unripe green papaya piece
4 tablespoons oil + for deep-frying
2 medium onions, sliced
2 tablespoons yogurt
1 teaspoon black pepper powder
1 teaspoon green cardamom powder
1 teaspoon *garam masala* powder
1 teaspoon lichen/stone flower powder
1 tablespoon malt vinegar
Salt to taste
Oil or ghee for basting

1. Pound the mutton with a steak hammer or the blunt side of a knife to make quarter-inch thick pieces. Grind the ginger, garlic, green chillies and papaya to a fine paste.

2. Heat the oil in a non-stick *kadai* and deep-fry the onions till brown. Drain, cool and grind with the yogurt to a fine paste.

3. Mix together the ground spice paste, onion-yogurt paste, pepper powder, cardamom powder, *garam masala* powder, lichen powder, malt vinegar and four tablespoons of oil. Coat the mutton pieces well with the mixture and leave to marinate for three or four hours, preferably in a refrigerator.

4. Take a flat slab of rough granite or *kadappa* stone that is about one and a half feet long, one foot wide and two-inch thick. Wash the stone and place it firmly on two piles of bricks. Light a charcoal fire underneath the stone slab and heat it well.

5. Season the stone by smearing it with oil when it is very hot. Sprinkle the stone with a little salt and wipe with a clean cloth. It is now ready to use. Sprinkle a little oil or ghee on the surface and place the marinated mutton pieces pasandey on the hot stone.

6. Turn the mutton pieces a few times, basting occasionally with oil. Remove when cooked through. Alternatively, the kababs can be cooked on a non-stick *tawa* over a gas flame. Serve with hot *tandoori roti* and Kachumber (page 95).

Boti Kabab

½ kg boneless mutton, cut into 1-inch cubes
2 tablespoons unripe papaya paste
1 tablespoon ginger paste
1 tablespoon garlic paste
½ teaspoon green chilli paste
½ teaspoon red chilli powder
¼ teaspoon *garam masala* powder
Salt to taste
¼ cup melted butter

1. Mix together the papaya paste, ginger paste, garlic paste, green chilli paste with the chilli powder, *garam masala* powder and salt and apply the marinade to the mutton cubes. Marinate for three to four hours, preferably in a refrigerator.
2. Pressure-cook the marinated mutton cubes with one cup of water till the pressure is released four times (four whistles) or till half-done. Remove the lid when the pressure reduces completely and check if there is any liquid remaining. If yes, then cook till all the water evaporates. Remove from the pressure cooker and set aside.
3. Heat a grill and grill the mutton cubes till completely cooked. Baste with melted butter from time to time so that the mutton does not dry out. Transfer to a plate and serve with onion rings and Mint Chutney (page 95).

Shaami Kabab

600 grams boneless mutton
½ cup split Bengal gram
2 medium onions, chopped
2 tablespoons chopped fresh coriander
2 tablespoons chopped fresh mint leaves
2 teaspoons lemon juice
3 tablespoons oil + for shallow-frying
½ teaspoon cumin seeds
1 teaspoon coriander seeds
5-6 black peppercorns
3-4 black cardamoms
2 inches ginger, finely chopped
10-12 garlic cloves, finely chopped
1 teaspoon red chilli powder
1 teaspoon *garam masala* powder
½ teaspoon mace powder
½ teaspoon green cardamom powder
Salt to taste
2 medium onions, cut into fine rings

1. Soak the split Bengal gram for at least three hours.
2. Mix together the onions, coriander, mint leaves and lemon juice to make a stuffing. Divide into sixteen equal portions and set aside.
3. Heat two tablespoons of oil in a pressure cooker; add the cumin seeds, coriander seeds, peppercorns, and black cardamoms and sauté for half a minute over medium heat. Add the ginger, garlic and chilli powder and sauté for a while.

4. Add the mutton and soaked Bengal gram, mix well, add two cups of water and bring to a boil. Cover the cooker and cook under pressure for about twenty-five minutes till pressure is released six times (six whistles). Remove the lid when the pressure has completely reduced. Cook over high heat to dry out the gravy completely, stirring continuously.
5. Remove from heat and set aside to cool. Process or grind the mixture till smooth.
6. Add the *garam masala* powder, mace and green cardamom powder and salt and mix well.
7. Divide the mixture into sixteen equal portions. Flatten each portion in the palm of your hand and place a portion of onion stuffing in the centre. Shape into balls and flatten slightly.
8. Heat the oil in a non-stick frying pan and shallow-fry the kababs till golden. Drain on absorbent paper. Serve hot with onion rings and Mint Chutney (page 95).

Chef's Tip: If the mutton mixture is too moist after cooking, add some roasted gram flour or powdered roasted split Bengal gram to correct the consistency.

Dum Ke Kabab

450 grams minced mutton
½ tablespoon unripe green papaya paste
Oil for deep-frying
2 medium onions, sliced
1 inch cinnamon
4 green cardamoms
3 cloves
½ teaspoon allspice
1 teaspoon melon seeds
½ teaspoon poppy seeds
3 dried red chillies, broken into pieces
½ teaspoon caraway seeds
3 green chillies
2 tablespoons chopped fresh coriander
4 garlic cloves
½ inch ginger
1½ teaspoons gram flour
1 tablespoon lemon juice
Salt to taste
½ cup yogurt, whisked
½ teaspoon red chilli powder
¼ teaspoon *garam masala* powder
1½ tablespoons pure ghee
1 medium onion, cut into rings
A few fresh mint sprigs
1 lemon, cut into wedges

1. Mix the green papaya paste into the minced mutton and leave to marinate for fifteen minutes. Grind till smooth.
2. Heat sufficient oil in a non-stick *kadai* and deep-fry the onions till golden. Drain on absorbent paper. Dry-roast the cinnamon, cardamoms, cloves and allspice separately till fragrant. Cool and grind together to a fine powder.
3. Dry-roast the melon seeds, poppy seeds, red chillies and caraway seeds separately till fragrant. Grind the spices together with the green chillies, fresh coriander, garlic and ginger to a smooth paste. Roast the gram flour over a low heat till fragrant. Mix all the spice powder, spice paste and the roasted gram flour with the minced mutton and grind till smooth. Transfer to a deep bowl.
4. Add the lemon juice and salt. Mix well. Cover the bowl with a cling film and place the mixture in the refrigerator for thirty minutes.
5. Preheat an oven to 220°C/ 425°F/Gas Mark 7. Whisk the yogurt with chilli powder and *garam masala* powder till well blended.
6. Divide the chilled mixture into twenty-four equal portions and shape into balls. Grease the palms of your hands with a little oil and shape the balls into sausages. Arrange on a greased tray and set aside.
7. Spoon a little of the yogurt mixture onto each kabab. Cook in the oven for twenty minutes, basting now and then with ghee every five minutes.
8. Remove from the oven and serve hot with onion rings, mint leaves and lemon wedges.

Seekh Kabab

500 grams minced mutton
50 grams mutton fat
1 medium onion, chopped
6 green chillies, chopped
2 tablespoons chopped fresh coriander
1 tablespoon garlic paste
1 tablespoon ginger paste
1 teaspoon roasted cumin powder
½ teaspoon *garam masala* powder
1 tablespoon Kashmiri chilli powder
Salt to taste
Oil or butter for basting
2 tablespoons *chaat masala*
2 lemons, to serve

1. Preheat an oven to 240°C/475°F/Gas Mark 9.
2. Mix together the minced mutton, mutton fat, onion, green chillies and chopped coriander. Grind to a fine consistency. Add the rest of the ingredients except the oil and mix well.
3. Divide the mixture into twelve equal portions. Pat the mince mixture with moist hands onto skewers and shape into kababs.
4. Cook the kababs in the preheated oven or in a hot *tandoor* till almost done. Baste with butter or oil and continue to cook till completely done. Sprinkle with a little *chaat masala* and lemon juice and serve hot with Mint Chutney (page 95).

Chef's Tip: Do not overcook the kababs – they should be moist and not dry.

Pasanda Kabab

750 grams boneless mutton, cut into 1½-inch cubes

Melted butter for basting

First Marinade

½ small unripe papaya, ground

Salt to taste

½ tablespoon white pepper powder

1 tablespoon ginger paste

1 tablespoon garlic paste

Second Marinade

150 grams cottage cheese, grated

2 tablespoons gram flour

1 egg white

½ cup cream

1 tablespoon cashew nut paste

½ tablespoon white pepper powder

½ teaspoon green cardamom powder

4 green chillies, finely chopped

1. Clean the mutton pieces, pat dry and flatten with the back of a knife.
2. For the first marinade, mix together the ground papaya, salt, white pepper powder, the ginger paste and garlic paste. Rub the mixture into the mutton cubes and set aside for an hour preferably, in a refrigerator.

3. For the second marinade, mix together the grated cottage cheese, gram flour and egg white in a bowl. Add the cream gradually and mix until well-blended.
4. Add the cashew nut paste, white pepper powder, cardamom powder and green chillies. Marinate the mutton in this mixture for at least five to six hours in the refrigerator.
5. Preheat the oven to 240°C/475°F/Gas Mark 9.
6. Thread the marinated mutton cubes onto skewers. Cook in the preheated oven or in a moderately hot *tandoor* for eight to ten minutes. Baste with melted butter and cook in the oven or *tandoor* for another three to four minutes.
7. Serve hot with Mint Chutney (page 95) and Kachumber (page 95).

Mutton Shaami Kabab

250 grams minced mutton
8 teaspoons oil + for deep-frying
1½ medium onions, chopped
2 tablespoons pure ghee
½ teaspoon caraway seeds
2 dried red chillies, broken
½ inch ginger, roughly chopped
5 garlic cloves, roughly chopped
1 tablespoon split Bengal gram, soaked for ½ hour
5 tablespoons chopped fresh mint
5 tablespoons chopped fresh coriander
½ tablespoon lemon juice
Salt to taste
1 egg, beaten

1. Heat sufficient oil in a non-stick *kadai* and deep-fry the onions till brown. Drain on absorbent paper.
2. Heat the ghee in a non-stick pan; add the caraway seeds, red chillies, ginger and garlic, and sauté for one minute.
3. Add the minced mutton and sauté for five minutes, stirring occasionally.
4. Drain the split Bengal gram and add to the pan. Stir and sauté for one minute.

5. Add the chopped mint and chopped coriander, and stir well. Cook for five minutes and set aside to cool.
6. Grind the mixture together with the fried onions, lemon juice and salt, to a coarse paste. Divide the paste into eight equal portions and shape into round patties and flatten slightly.
7. Heat two teaspoons oil in a shallow non-stick pan. Dip two kababs in the beaten egg and shallow-fry for three or four minutes till golden brown on both sides.
8. Serve hot with Mint Chutney (page 95) and onion rings.

Galouti Kabab

250 grams minced mutton
20 cashew nuts
5 tablespoons oil + for deep-frying
2 small onions, sliced
3½ tablespoons unripe papaya paste
2 tablespoons + 1 teaspoon ghee
⅓ teaspoon roasted split Bengal gram powder
½ teaspoon red chilli powder
1½ teaspoons salt
5 tablespoons pure ghee
1 piece of charcoal

Galouti Masala
2 blades of mace
4 inches cinnamon
14 cloves
A pinch of allspice
1 gram rose petals
13 green cardamom
A generous pinch of saffron

1. Heat one tablespoon oil in a non-stick frying pan; add the cashew nuts and sauté, stirring continuously, till golden. Drain on absorbent paper and set aside to cool. Transfer to a blender jar and grind to a powder.

2. Heat sufficient oil in a non-stick *kadai*; add the onions and cook till golden brown. Drain on an absorbent paper. Cool and transfer into a blender jar and blend into a paste.
3. To make the galouti *masala*, place a small non-stick pan on medium heat for two minutes, reduce the heat to low, add mace, cinnamon, ten cloves, allspice, rose petals and green cardamoms and roast for thirty seconds. Set aside to cool. Transfer into a blender jar and blend to a fine powder. Similarly lightly roast the saffron for ten seconds and pound to a powder.
4. Wash the ground mutton and drain well in a colander. Transfer the ground mutton into a mincer jar. Add the cashew nut powder, browned onion paste, unripe papaya paste and roasted gram powder and mince till all the ingredients are well blended and form a smooth paste.
5. Add the chilli powder, the roasted and ground spices, saffron and salt and blend again.
6. Transfer the mutton mixture onto a plate and rub in the mixture well with the heel of your palm for two to three minutes. Add the ghee, reserving one teaspoon for smoking, and rub it in for two to three minutes more or till the ghee is well incorporated into the mixture.
7. Gather the mixture into the centre of the plate. Make a hollow in the centre and place a small stainless steel bowl. Heat the coal on open flame till red hot and place it in the bowl. Place

four cloves over it and drizzle the reserved ghee over it. Immediately cover the plate with aluminium foil and let it rest for fifteen to twenty minutes.

8. Cover the plate with cling film and place it in the refrigerator to chill for one hour.
9. Remove the plate from the refrigerator and divide the mixture into sixteen equal portions and shape into patties.
10. Place a medium non-stick frying pan on medium heat and pour in four tablespoons oil; place the kababs, four at a time, and cook, turning sides once, till both the sides are golden.
11. Drain onto an absorbent paper and serve hot.

Keema Tikki Kabab

400 grams minced mutton
100 grams mutton fat
2 medium onions, chopped
3-4 green chillies, chopped
4 sprigs fresh coriander leaves, chopped
1 tablespoon garlic paste
1 tablespoon ginger paste
1 teaspoon cumin powder
1 teaspoon *garam masala* powder
2 teaspoons Kashmiri chilli powder
Salt to taste
½ cup oil
2 teaspoons *chaat masala*
2 teaspoons lemon juice

1. Grind the lamb mince, mutton fat, onion, green chillies and chopped coriander twice, until smooth. Mix in the garlic paste, ginger paste, cumin powder, *garam masala* powder, chilli powder and salt to taste.
2. Divide the mince mixture into sixteen equal portions. Shape into one-inch round and half-inch thick patties and place on a baking tray. Grill for fifteen to twenty minutes, turning over once and brushing with oil every five minutes to get an even brown crust.
3. Serve hot, sprinkled with *chaat masala* and lemon juice.

Chef's Tip: For tender, succulent kababs, add some green, unripe papaya or pineapple paste to the minced mutton.

BASIC RECIPES

Pineapple Chutney

Peel and cut 1 medium pineapple into small pieces and place in a thick-bot tomed pan. Add 1 teaspoon ginger paste, mix well and cook for 5 minutes. Add 1 tablespoon sugar and 2 tablespoons raisins and cook. Add ½ teaspoon roasted *panch phoron* powder, ½ teaspoon crushed red chillies and salt to taste. Add ½ cup water and cook for 5 minutes on low heat. Sprinkle ½ teaspoon roasted *panch phoron* powder and serve.

Note: *Panch phoron* is a mixture of ¼ teaspoon mustard seeds, ¼ teaspoon cumin seeds, ¼ teaspoon fenugreek seeds, ¼ teaspoon fennel seeds and ¼ teaspoon onion seeds.

Mint Chutney

Grind 5 cups mint leaves, 3 cups coriander leaves, 10 green chillies, 3 onions, and 3 inches of ginger to a fine paste, adding a little water if required. Stir in 1 tablespoon lemon juice, salt and pomegranate seed powder to taste.

Kachumber

Cut 1 medium tomato, 1 medium cucumber, 1 medium green capsicum, ½ medium white radish and 1 medium carrot, into ½-inch pieces. Mix the vegetables in a bowl and add 1 chopped medium onion, 2 chopped green chillies, 2 tablespoons chopped fresh coriander, 1 tablespoon lemon juice and salt to taste. Toss well. Transfer to a salad bowl and serve cold.

GLOSSARY

English	Hindi
Allspice	Kababchini
Baby corn	Chhote makai
Bengal gram, split	Chana dal
Bengal gram, split roasted	Daalia
Butter	Makkhan
Caraway seeds	Shahi jeera
Cardamoms, black	Badi elaichi
Cardamoms, green	Chhoti elaichi
Carom seeds	Ajwain
Chilli, fresh red	Taazi lal mirch
Cinnamon	Dalchini
Coriander seeds	Sabut dhania
Cudpahnut	Chironji
Dried fenugreek leaves	Kasuri methi
Dried mango powder	Amchur
French beans	Farsi
Lichen/stone flower	Pathher ke phool

English	Hindi
Mace	Javitri
Mushroom	Khumb
Nutmeg	Jaiphal
Olives	Jaitun
Peppercorns	Kali mirch
Pomegranate seeds, dried	Ananrdana
Poppy seeds	Khuskhus
Refined flour	Maida
Saffron	Kesar
Sandalwood	Chandan
Screw pine	Kewda
Shallots	Chhote pyaaz
Turmeric powder	Haldi
Vinegar	Sirka
Yam	Suran
Yogurt	Dahi